Moya and Mindy The Mermaid Adventures

This Is Moya.

She loves mermaids
and dreams about
them very often.

As Moya wakes up, she can tell this is going to be a great day.

"Time to get these teeth clean" Moya said as she brushed her teeth.

"Now for a good bath", She said as she played with her rubber duck in the bubbles.

Moya loved to have
her breakfast outside
in the open air.

Dolly, her little brown
puppy, enjoyed the
outdoors too.

Moya also loved
watching her mother
do her morning yoga
sessions on the
grass.

After breakfast, Moya
took Dolly to the
beach, which was
close to their home.

As Dolly and Moya watched the happy Dolphins play in the ocean, little did they know the surprise that was about to unfold.

Right below the ocean
was a beautiful
mermaid called
Mindy.

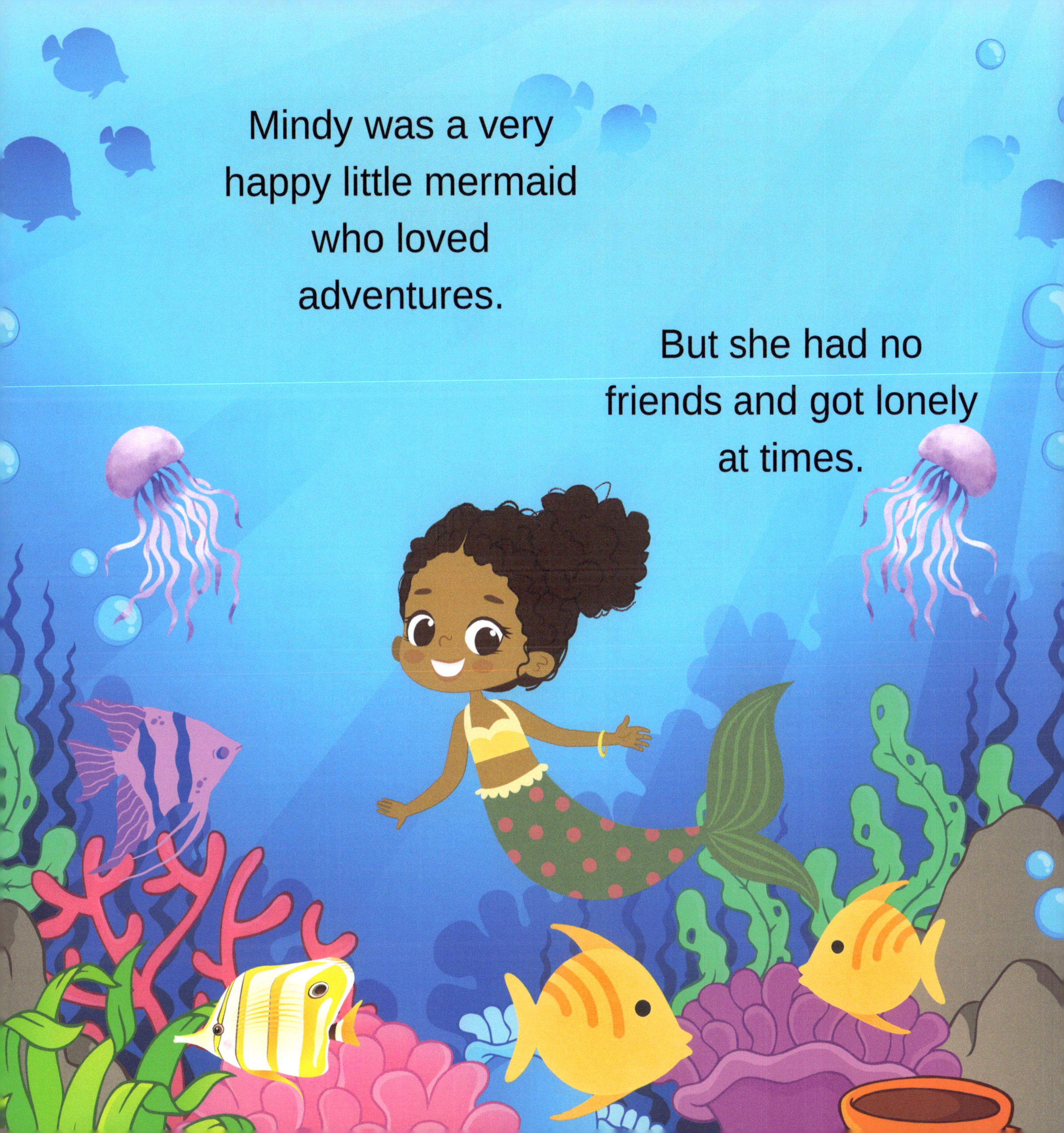

Mindy was a very happy little mermaid who loved adventures.
But she had no friends and got lonely at times.

Just as Moya was
about to head home
with Dolly, her little
brown puppy.

She saw Mindy
appear from the
surface of the ocean.

Moya was shocked.

She tried to talk, but no words came out of her lips, she could not believe her eyes. Was she dreaming?

"Hello there!" said Mindy.

"My name is Mindy and I am a mermaid from the Shell's Mermaid Kingdom".

"What's your name?"
she asked Moya.

As Moya managed to
pull herself together,
she replied, "my name
is Moya and I am from
earth".

Mindy laughed at Moya's reply. "I am not an alien if that is what you think Moya but it is nice to meet you".

Moya laughed, she thought Mindy the mermaid was very funny.

"I never thought I would ever see a real live mermaid," said Moya.

"I love mermaids and often dream of them".

"Do you live around
here?" Mindy asked.

"Yes, I live very close
by" Moya answered.

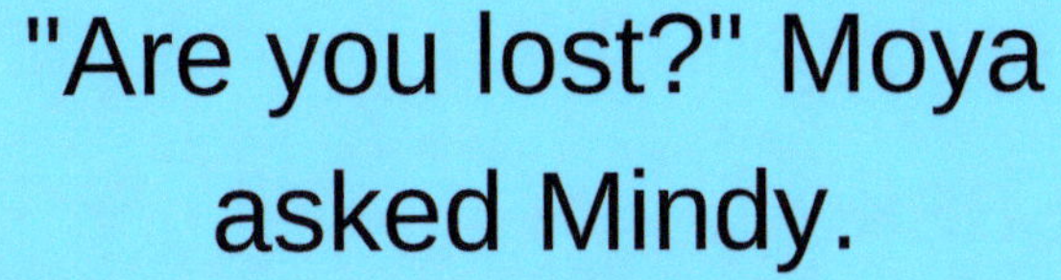

"Are you lost?" Moya
asked Mindy.

"Not really" Mindy
answered. "I often
leave the kingdom to
go on adventures".

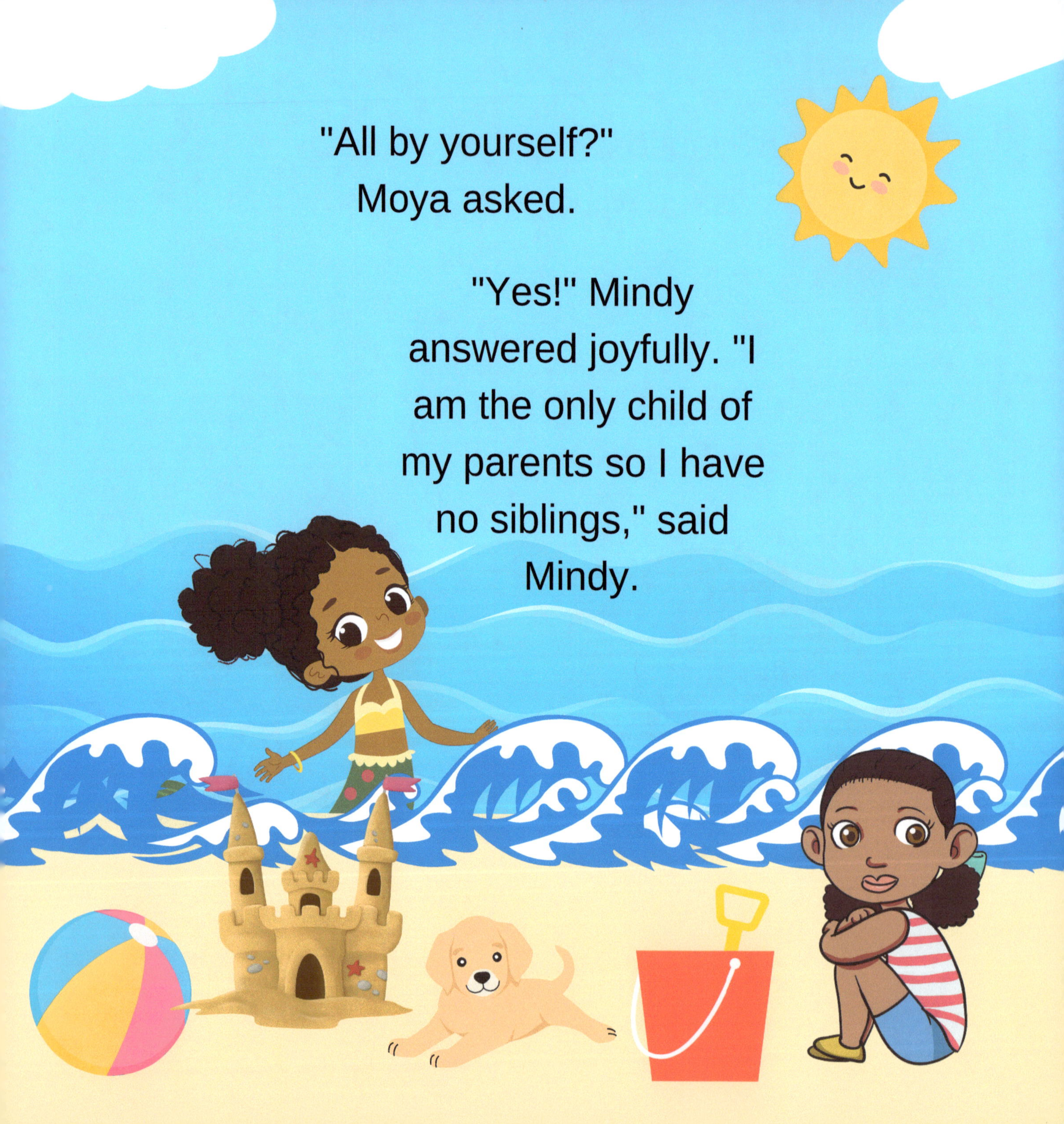

"All by yourself?"
Moya asked.

"Yes!" Mindy
answered joyfully. "I
am the only child of
my parents so I have
no siblings," said
Mindy.

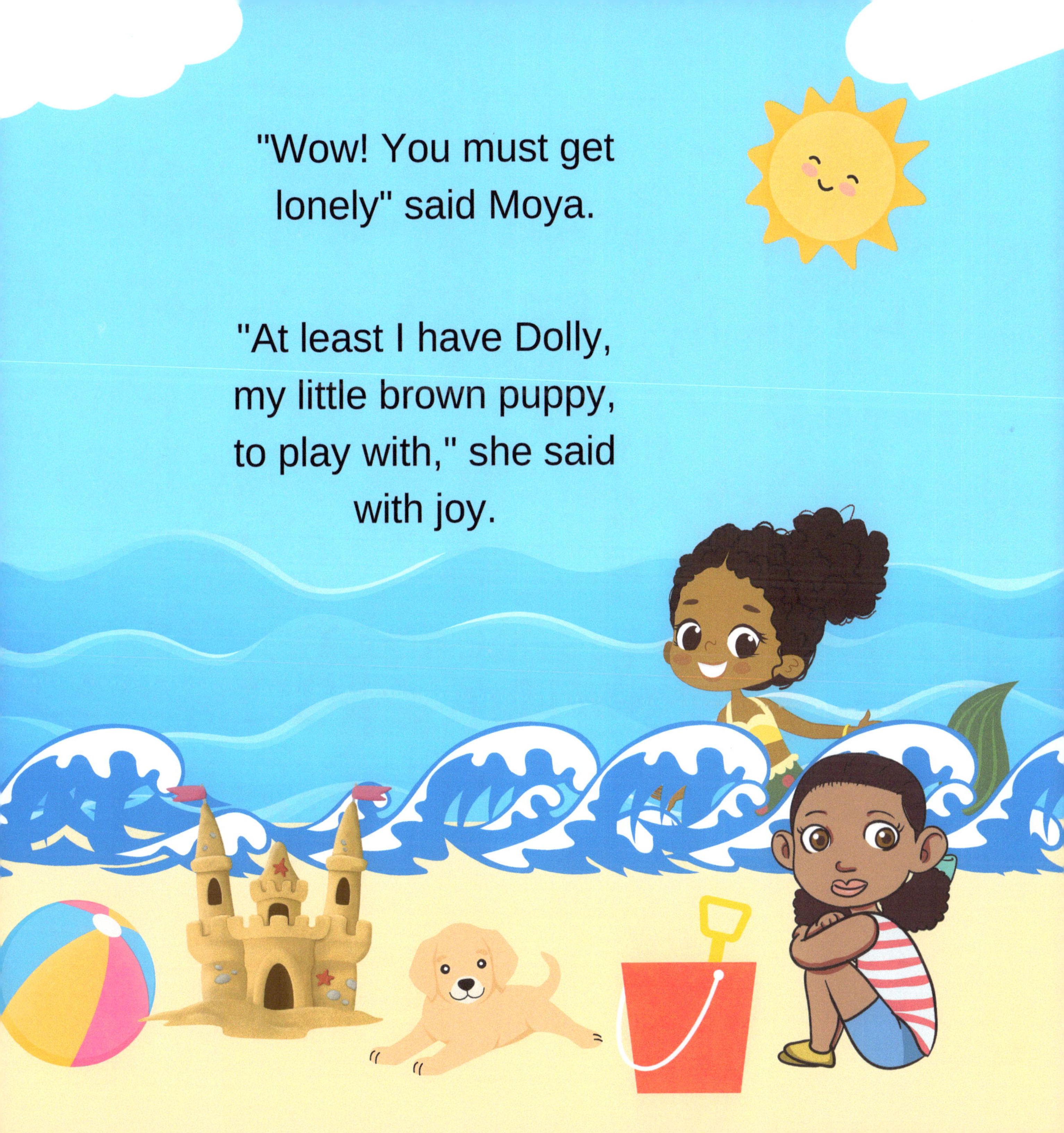

"Wow! You must get
lonely" said Moya.

"At least I have Dolly,
my little brown puppy,
to play with," she said
with joy.

"Your puppy is very cute," said Mindy.

"Don't you have any siblings?" she asked Moya.

"I don't" Moya
answered.

"We can be friends,"
Mindy said excitedly.

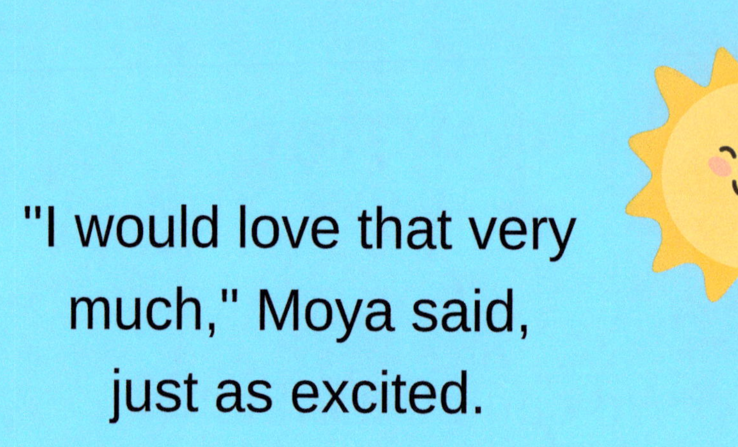

"I would love that very
much," Moya said,
just as excited.

"Would you like to go
on an adventure,
Moya?" Mindy asked.

"Of course!" Moya
answered, "But how?"

"Leave that to me"
Mindy answered. "We
are going to have so
much fun together".

Mindy waved a wand
and suddenly Moya
had a mermaid tail.

Mindy took Moya under the ocean and they both had so much fun swimming around the ocean.

"Wow!" Moya said, "I can't believe my dreams of swimming with a mermaid is coming through.

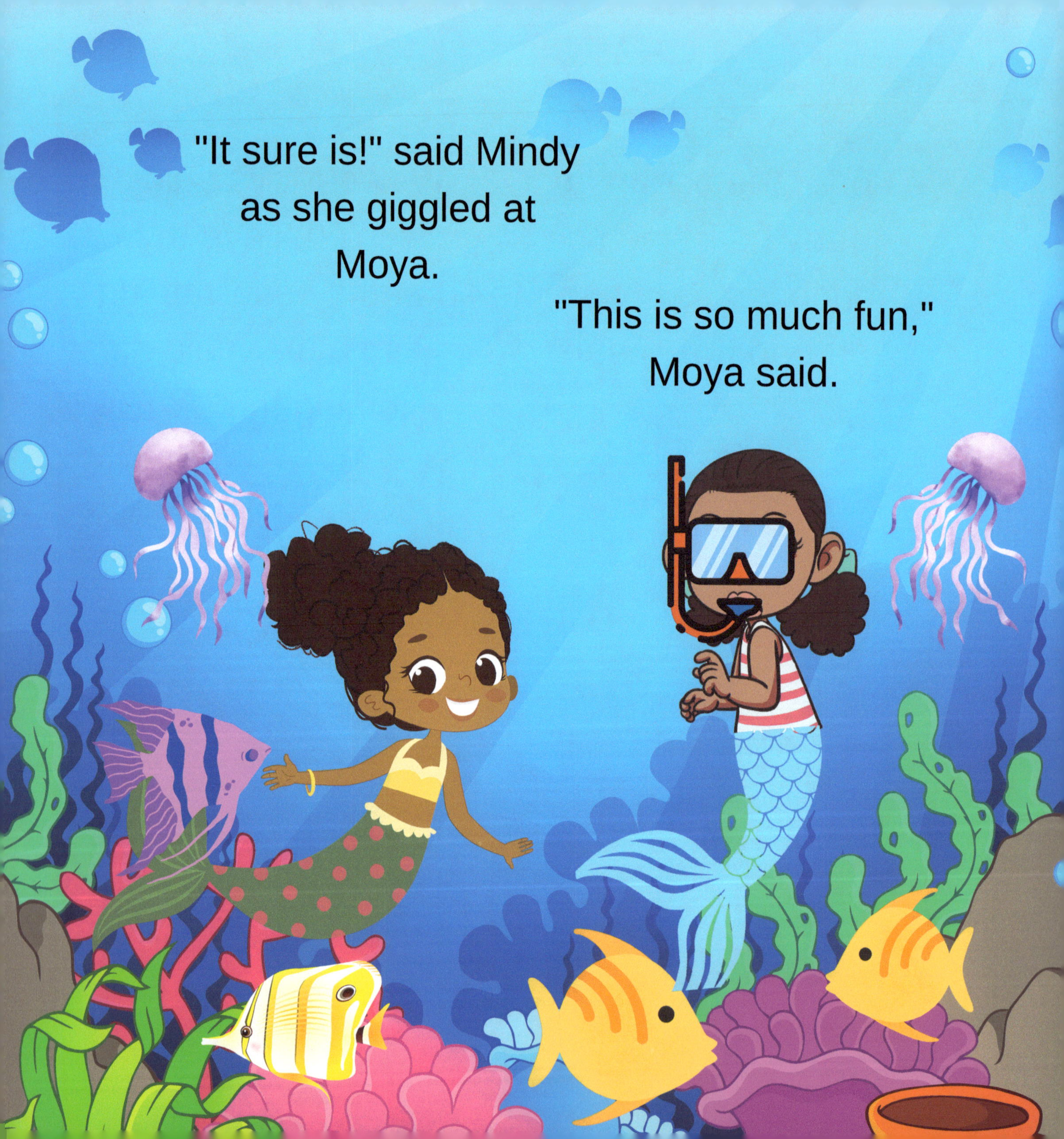

"It sure is!" said Mindy as she giggled at Moya.

"This is so much fun," Moya said.

Moya found a beautiful purple seashell.

She had never seen a purple seashell before.

Moya met an octopus
for the very first time,
he was very friendly
but shy.

She also met Mr.
Crab, who was very
funny and made her
laugh so much.

Mindy knew that
Moya was having fun,
but it was getting late
and she knew it was
time to take her
home.

"Come on Moya, it is time to go, it is getting late" Mindy said.

Moya wanted to stay longer but she knew Mindy was right, and her mom may be looking for her.

"See you tomorrow Moya," Mindy said," it was great swimming with you under the sea".

"Thank you, my new friend, Mindy: Moya replied.

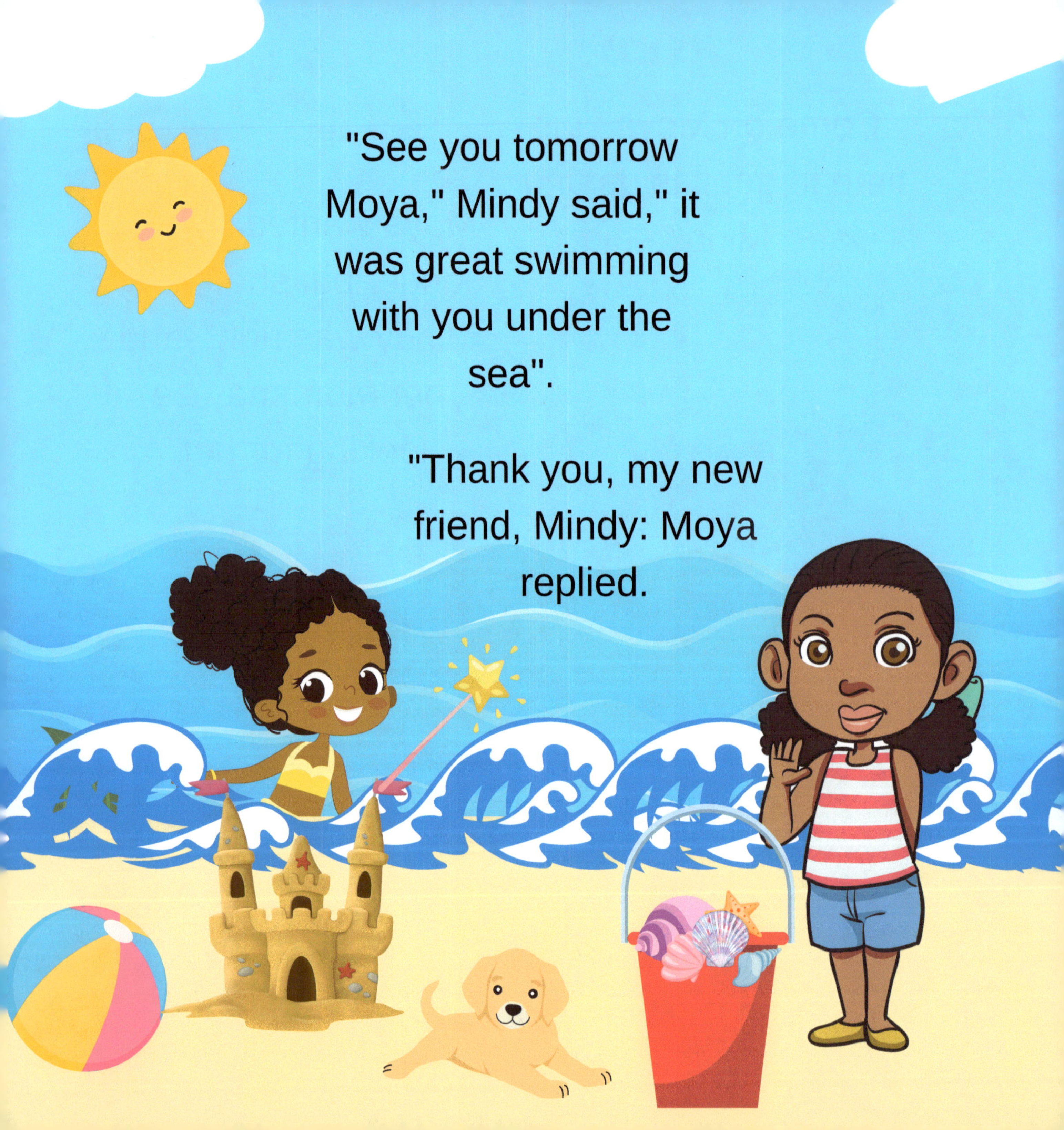

As Moya waved
goodbye to Mindy,
she felt a sense of
accomplishment.

"My dreams have
come through," she
said to herself, "but
who will believe me?"

"Well, I have these
very unusual beautiful
seashells as proof,"
she thought.

"I can't wait to tell my
mom and friends
about my adventure
with my new friend,
Mindy the mermaid".

Sure enough, that night Moya dreamt of mermaids.

This time, though, she did not just dream of any mermaid.

She dreamt of her new friend Mindy, the beautiful mermaid.

Moya couldn't wait to go on another adventure with Mindy again.